AMERICAN HEROES

GEORGE WASHINGTON CARVER

INVENTOR AND ACTIVIST

by Katie Chanez

I0605925

pogo

Pogo Books, an imprint of Jump! Library by FlutterBee

Ideas for Parents and Teachers

Pogo Books let children practice reading informational text while introducing them to nonfiction features such as headings, labels, sidebars, maps, and diagrams, as well as a table of contents, glossary, and index.

Carefully leveled text with a strong photo match offers early fluent readers the support they need to succeed.

Before Reading

- "Walk" through the book and point out the various nonfiction features. Ask the student what purpose each feature serves.
- Look at the glossary together. Read and discuss the words.

During Reading

- Have the child read the book independently.
- Invite them to list questions that arise from reading.

After Reading

- Discuss the child's questions. Talk about how they might find answers to those questions.
- Prompt the child to think more. Ask: Did you know about George Washington Carver before reading this book? What more would you like to learn about his life?

Pogo Books are published by Jump!
3500 American Blvd W, Suite 150
Bloomington, MN 55431
www.jumplibrary.com

Jump! is a division of FlutterBee Education Group.

Library of Congress Cataloging-in-Publication Data is available at www.loc.gov or upon request from the publisher.

ISBN: 979-8-89662-358-8 (hardcover)
ISBN: 979-8-89662-359-5 (paperback)
ISBN: 979-8-89662-360-1 (ebook)

Editor: Alyssa Sorenson
Designer: Molly Ballanger

Photo Credits: AP Images, cover, 10; Library of Congress, 1, 5, 10-11; PW.Stocker/Adobe Stock, 3; Anthony Barboza/Getty, 4; Danita Delimont/Adobe Stock, 6-7; Paul R. Burley/Wikimedia, 8; Iowa State University, Special Collections and University Archives, 9 (foreground); Pixel-Shot/Adobe Stock, 9 (background); zhang yongxin/Adobe Stock, 12-13; National Archives, 14-15, 16-17; Stock Montage/Getty, 18; Hulton-Deutsch Collection/Corbis/Getty, 19; National Park Service, 20-21; Mccallk69/Shutterstock, 21; Zack Frank/Adobe Stock, 23.

Printed in the United States of America at Corporate Graphics in North Mankato, Minnesota.

TABLE OF CONTENTS

CHAPTER 1

EARLY LIFE

George Washington Carver was born around 1864. He was born into **slavery**. When he was a baby, George's mother and sister were taken. He never saw them again. This was hard for George. But he grew up to be a famous scientist.

George was born near Diamond, Missouri. He lived on Moses and Susan Carver's farm. They were white. In 1865, the American Civil War ended. New laws made slavery **illegal**.

Carver house

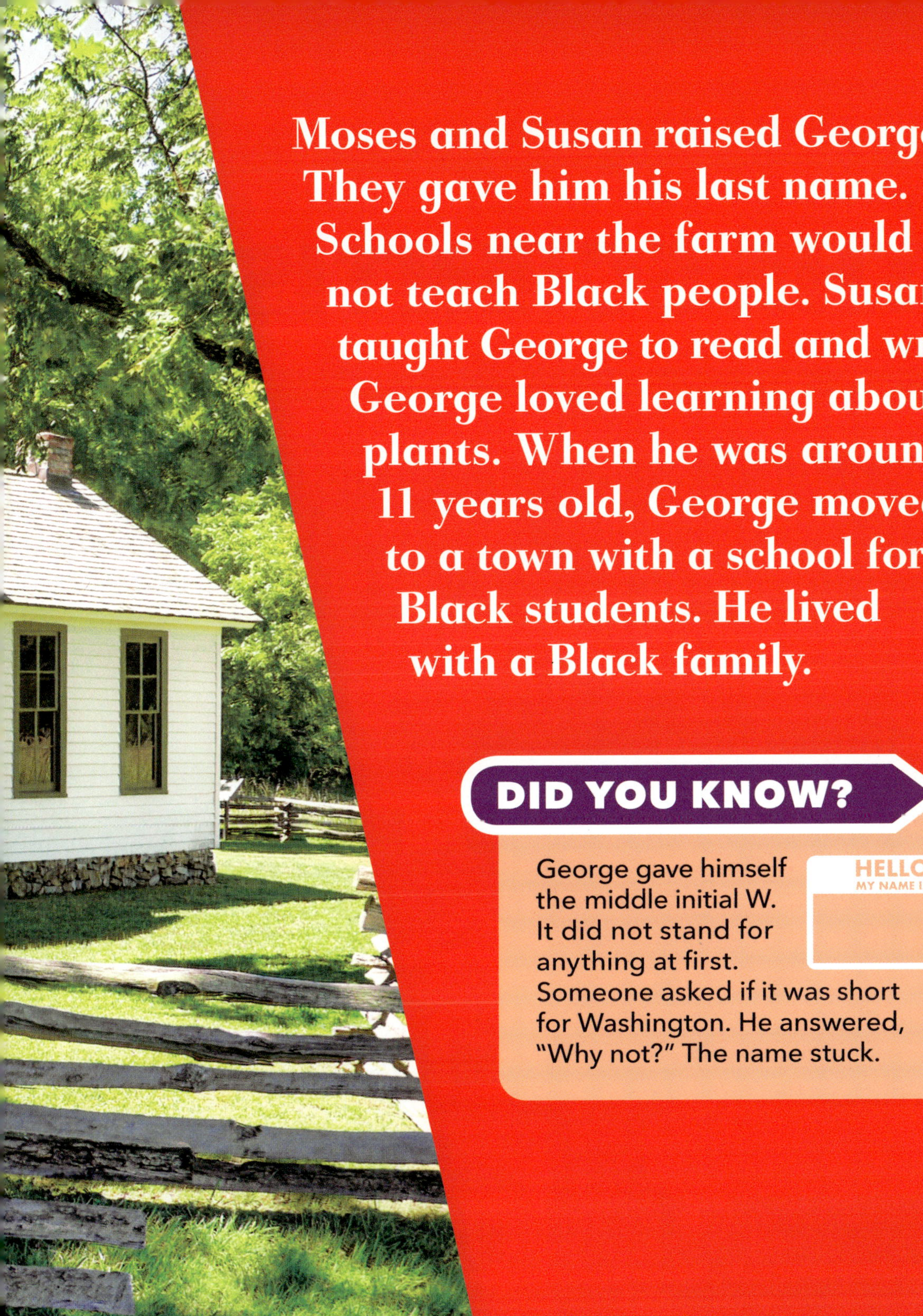

Moses and Susan raised George. They gave him his last name. Schools near the farm would not teach Black people. Susan taught George to read and write. George loved learning about plants. When he was around 11 years old, George moved to a town with a school for Black students. He lived with a Black family.

DID YOU KNOW?

George gave himself the middle initial W. It did not stand for anything at first. Someone asked if it was short for Washington. He answered, "Why not?" The name stuck.

CHAPTER 2

THE SCIENTIST

George did well in school. After high school, he was going to go to Highland **College** in Kansas. But the school changed its mind. Why? It found out George was Black. In 1890, George went to Simpson College in Iowa instead. This school taught Black and white students.

Simpson College

Iowa State University

George studied piano and art. He often made drawings and paintings of plants. His art teacher suggested he study **botany**. George left Simpson. He went to what is now Iowa State University. He learned more about botany. He was the first Black student there.

Then he went to Alabama. In 1896, he began teaching at the Tuskegee Institute. This is a college for Black students. George spent the next 47 years there! He taught. He **researched** plants, too.

George

At this time, many farmers in southern states only grew cotton. This caused the soil to lose **nutrients**. George suggested **crop rotation**. Farmers could plant different crops. The new crops would help bring back nutrients. These new crops included sweet potatoes, peanuts, pecans, and soybeans.

TAKE A LOOK!

How does crop rotation work? Take a look!

Not many people bought the new crops. That did not stop George. He **invented** hundreds of **products** that used them. He made new types of **fuel**, paint, and more! Farmers could sell their crops to make these products.

WHAT DO YOU THINK?

George invented more than 300 uses for peanuts, 100 for sweet potatoes, and 75 for pecans! What would you like to invent? Why?

Jesup wagon
THE JESUP AGRICULTURAL WAGON

In 1906, George created the Jesup wagon. It was a classroom that could move. He used it to travel to farmers. He shared what he learned with them!

WHAT DO YOU THINK?

Imagine you had your own Jesup wagon. What would you teach? Who would you teach it to?

CHAPTER 3

LATER LIFE

George became a speaker and **activist**. In the 1920s, he visited colleges in the South. He spoke about education. He said everyone deserved to learn, no matter their **race**.

During George's lifetime, few Black people were respected by white Americans. But George became famous. He was a **spokesman** for the United Peanut Associations of America. He spoke about the many uses of peanuts. He talked to **Congress** about the importance of peanuts. He even met President Franklin D. Roosevelt!

Franklin D. Roosevelt

George died on January 5, 1943. He is remembered. There is a **monument** for him in Diamond. It reminds people of his life and work. George changed farming forever! Many schools and museums are named after him.

QUICK FACTS & TOOLS

TIMELINE

What are big events in George Washington Carver's life? Take a look!

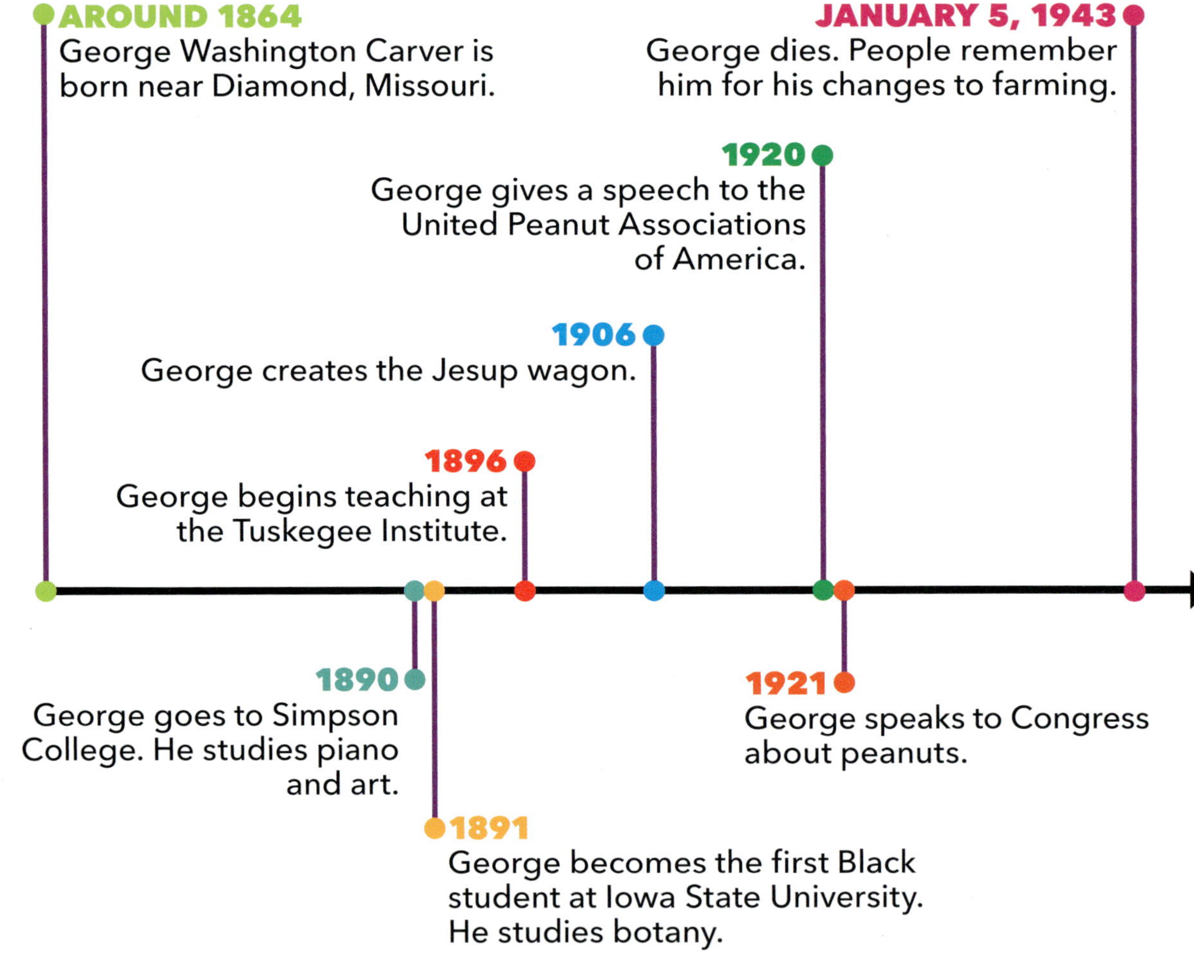

GLOSSARY

activist: A person who supports a cause and believes in taking action to change things.

botany: The study of plant life.

college: A place that teaches higher learning beyond high school.

Congress: The part of the U.S. government that makes laws.

crop rotation: The practice of growing different crops one after another to protect the soil.

fuel: Something that is used as a source of heat or energy, such as coal, wood, or gasoline.

illegal: Against the law.

invented: Created something new.

monument: A statue, building, or other structure that reminds people of a person or event.

nutrients: Substances that people and animals need to stay strong and healthy.

products: Things that are manufactured or made by natural process.

race: A group that people are divided into based on their appearance.

researched: Collected information through reading, investigating, or experimenting.

slavery: The practice of forcing people to work in harsh conditions with no pay.

spokesman: A person who speaks on behalf of someone else or a group.

INDEX

TO LEARN MORE

Finding more information is as easy as 1, 2, 3.

1. Go to www.factsurfer.com
2. Enter "George Washington Carver" into the search box.
3. Choose your book to see a list of websites.